POMPIDOU CENTER

to Mes Carol Royal
in friendship and
esteem

Ivan Zaknic

Princeton, May 25. 88

POMPIDOU CENTER

Photography by Jeremiah Bragstad
Text by Ivan Žaknić
Preface by Renzo Piano

FLAMMARION

Contents

Preface

It was in the five years between 1971 and 1977 that we built Centre Pompidou—Richard Rogers, our team and myself, with Peter Rice and other friends of Ove Arup and Partners.

It was a great adventure, as much on the technical level as on the human: the relationship with the contractors and with technology, as well as with the people and the city of Paris.

Our goal was to knock down the wall of mistrust which has always separated the general public from official culture; it was equally to reject all institutionalized relationships and to provoke in people curiosity, awakening their consciousness concerning events, arousing in them a curiosity so often dormant since childhood.

On the functional level, this building allowed for honest expression by its rejection of the idea of elite culture, replacing intimidation by inquisitiveness.

On the technical and architectural level, our project was also to be an experiment provocative as an idea of a "factory" for disseminating information and knowledge.

On the functional as well as architectural level, the result is, perhaps, for the cultural establishment a sign of crisis.

But we had so much fun building it, piece by piece and day by day, that we certainly deserve some indulgence!

Renzo Piano

Introduction

THE NATIONAL CENTER OF ART & CULTURE, GEORGES POMPIDOU

Anyone visiting Paris cannot miss it—the remarkable 21st-century National Center of Art & Culture, Georges Pompidou. Is this building a monster, a superb work of architecture, or a new and high level of artistic and technological achievement?

Paris has been for a long time preeminently the city of pleasure, the cradle of all the newest in fashion, luxury and ideas. The latest jewel in its center is a contribution of France's late President, Georges Pompidou. It is one of the most extraordinary cultural enterprises undertaken in the history of France. Pompidou was the only French president who dared to transform the presidential Elysée Palace into a showcase for modern art and decor. For the new National Art Center, he seized the opportunity to build on an available parcel of undeveloped land in an area of Paris known as Plateau Beaubourg. In 1969 Pompidou called for an open international competition in which 49 countries participated and 681 designs were presented. In 1971 an international jury designated the winners: the Italian-English architectural team of Piano and Rogers. The architects described their design as a place of constantly changing information—a cross between multi-media oriented Times Square and a sober British Museum. "Ça va faire crier" (It will make for a lot of shouting), predicted Pompidou, knowing that Parisians would be highly critical of its strong and unusual presence. He could not have been more correct.

Today the result, which cost about $200 million, stands in the heart of Paris on the Right Bank. 166 meters long, 60 meters wide and 42 meters high, it soars above the rooftops of Paris with its exposed mechanical entrails and structural skeleton. Parisians refer to it as the "refinery," the "distillery," the "ocean liner," the "Pompidolium," or simply Beaubourg.

The building is basically conceived as a huge glass box held up by an exterior steel scaffolding. All the parts which are usually hidden inside a

building have here been exposed on the outside, calling attention to their function. In comparison to its neighbors, the 17th and 18th century apartment houses in the area, it is not a dominant building in terms of size. But it stands in stunning contrast to them, especially at night, when it looks like a space machine that has landed on the public square. Over half of the site on which it stands has been left as an open square for a variety of spontaneous public events and street festivals so dear to the French people.

Ever since the Centre opened its doors in February 1977, huge crowds have poured into it to learn, to participate, to intermingle with others, or simply to be amazed. During the first five months of its existence, Centre Pompidou attracted more visitors than do the Louvre and Napoleon's Tomb combined for an entire year. Originally, the staff of the Centre optimistically predicted a turnout of 10,000 visitors a day; a year later they could not cope with crowds of 26,000 to 30,000 daily. This is the best equipped modern facility

the French capital has ever seen, and its most unusual structure since the Eiffel Tower was built in 1889. The Eiffel Tower was also considered a "horror," a monument to bad taste, even by the most prominent artists, writers and architects of the time.

As a monument not only to art but also to contemporary building techniques and technology, the Centre makes an awesome impression. Facing the Rue Renard on the East Side, the building has been aligned with others along the sidewalk and shows you its technological side, its "anatomical systems." All the services are exposed and color coded. The other side faces an open public square and is the principle approach from the west side. Here escalators lead you to different levels and skywalks to the roof top through a plastic tubular passageway that looks like a rollercoaster. This multi-disciplinary Centre is much more than a museum. It has three other major areas: the Public Library, the Industrial Age Design Center, and the Music Research Center.

The Plan and Development

Beaubourg's Role and Raison d'Etre

In 1977 part of Paris suddenly moved into the future with a single building, a gigantic assemblage of steel and glass. As President Pompidou said five years earlier: ''I would passionately love for Paris to have a cultural center that is both a museum and a center of creation, where the plastic arts would be side by side with music, cinema, books and audiovisual research.'' This center was a visionary thought, but it had a sound practical base. The cultural centers of France were scattered throughout the country and the capital; Pompidou was sensitive to Paris' need to provide its citizens with badly-needed cultural facilities. There was no precedent in France for a complex building of this kind, and this made the undertaking both risky and experimental. Administrative approval for this kind of project was not easy to achieve, especially when large sums of public

11

money had to be spent. Pompidou was a masterful politician, weaving his way between two dangerous extremes: the possibility of criticism and scandal if control guidelines were not provided, and the knowledge that too many restrictions would be harmful and perhaps even kill the project.

In addition, the building of a huge cultural center in Paris triggered an old debate: should the public money alloted to culture be consumed entirely in Paris, or should attempts be made to de-centralize culture and support smaller centers in the provinces? With his new plan, Pompidou chose to bring all France to Paris, but, as we shall see, provisions were also made in the new Centre for travelling exhibitions, pre-packaged and distributed to the provinces.

There were also problems in the French architectural scene, both in training and in practice. Contemporary architecture in France had become a mere imitation of American models. The Architecutre Department at the Beaux Arts School kept its students out of touch with new techniques and methods, and commissions and teaching positions were usually given to the same limited number of established architects—thus denying newcomers any opportunity to express their creative ideas.

This was the climate and the context in which President Pompidou, a connoisseur of contemporary art, stepped forward with his plan to build a large and modern national center. Fortunately, there was an available site on Plateau Beaubourg, situated between Les Halles and the historical Marrais District, which had been vacant since the 1930s, when a large section of decayed apartment buildings had been torn down.

The decision to locate the Centre in the very heart of Paris was both daring and practical. President Pompidou himself said that Beaubourg had been chosen because it was the only site available at the time, and he wanted the project

Photograph by Marc Riboud

to proceed with no delays.

"Le Plateau Beaubourg," in French "the beautiful borough," had for more than thirty years been used as a parking lot. Its history is one of dense growth and continual urban renewal. The fourth arrondissement or ward, in which it is located, is one of the most populated districts of Paris. The revolutions and cholera plagues in 1832 and 1871 encouraged the clearing of buildings and the laying out of new, straight and wider streets. This began under the Second Empire and continued during the Third Republic. A series of "major surgeries" were carried out on this area in the nineteenth century, including the most famous by Baron Haussmann: wide, straight boulevards were cut through the district. In the 1920s and 1930s, the area contained mostly small businesses, artisans, some intellectuals, and many workers, both foreign and French, many living in substandard housing. The block on which the Centre stands today was demolished in 1934-36, for fear that rats would cause an epidemic. There was even fear of plague. The demolition necessary for the Beaubourg Project in the 1970s, then, was a relatively minor job: a few old houses, and one magnificent private hotel dating from the seventeenth century.

For one hundred years, the area has had a tradition of reconstruction. But with this latest project, Beaubourg became for the first time a thoroughly enjoyable pedestrian district. It fits into a larger demographic pattern affecting all of Paris. Paris has always been a city that attracts residents to its center. There was a period when the middle and upper classes moved to the suburbs, but during the ten years preceding Pompidou's project, many were moving back to the center city to avoid the daily harassment of commuting. A central site for the new cultural project would be the most convenient for all classes of French citizens.

After the demolition of Les Halles in the early 1970s and the building of the Centre, the social and economic profile of the area changed. Many small art galleries and antique shops opened; restaurants and bookshops appeared; housing was restored and new units built. Through zoning ordinances, the authorities responsible for the Centre also control development in the immediate area.

The architects were, from the very beginning, concerned with a larger area than the building itself. They planned and fought for a series of open spaces along the pedestrian axis, to enrich the experience of approaching the Centre from various angles and perspectives. Its setting and ideology are in many ways similar to a medieval town, with street mazes leading to the Cathedral square via many smaller squares and innumerable complementary "events." A great deal of space was saved by burying one of the four major tenants of the Centre, the Music Research Center, underground next to the main building. The open public square, called "Place Igor Stravinsky," is left for the pedestrian to enjoy. Thus, the site is, despite its super-modern structure, being used in quite a traditional way.

The Evolution of Beaubourg's Program

For ten years before its opening, hundreds of individuals participated in developing the concepts, planning the program, and realizing the structure. By 1971 there was not yet a clearly defined program, but there was a committee of fifteen members (architects, engineers and administrators) responsible for defining a future program.

The committee discussed the future departments of the new Centre, each of which was to

Photograph on the next page by Gene Fenn

Multi-colored pipes along rue de Renard: more than a simple decoration, they are a display of form and function. Red is for vertical transportation, green for water, blue for air-conditioning, yellow for electricity, and the huge white ducts for ventilating the underground areas. Opposite page: the bus stop and entry to Centre Pompidou from the street.

have its own statute. These departments were to be:

1. *The National Museum of Modern Art*, which was to have the status of a National Museum under the authority of the director of Museums of France.

2. *The Public Information Library,* at this time called Bibliothèque des Halles, because it was to be built on this site as the Central Market pavilions were torn down. It was already temporarily occu-pying Pavilion No. 1 of the Central Markets, built by Baltard in the 1850s. It had a personnel of forty members.

3. *The Industrial Age Design Center*. It was not yet officially defined as a department, but grew out of the Central Union of the Decorative Arts of the Louvre. It was incorporated into the program for the Centre in 1974.

4. *The Music Research Center*, conceived by Pierre Boulez as a laboratory for contemporary

music. In February 1974, Boulez announced to the Press his creation of the center, and undertook its direction with an autonomous statute.

By 1971, then, the four major departments were either in the process of being defined, or had already been formed out of earlier organizations. This was only two years after the President of the Republic had expressed his initial desire to create a national center. By 1972, a provisional budget had been prepared, taking into consideration the projected needs of each department, and it was first approved by the Department of Cultural Affairs, and then by the Treasury Department. In order to insure closer cooperation, in 1972 the representatives of these four departments moved to temporary barracks on the construction site and, later, to a building adjacent to the site. This move was vital for the future development of the program, which continued to evolve throughout the construction of the building. In the meantime other services were added: an Audio-Visual Center, a Catalogues and Editing Printing Center to serve inter-departmental communication needs, Personnel and Legal Services, and in 1975 a children's workshop. To insure a smooth transition, and to avoid creating a gap between what was expected and what was actually provided in the new Center, displays by the different departments were presented to the public under the sponsorship of Centre Beaubourg—demonstrating its existence and unity even before the building was erected. These displays served a second purpose: to appease public opinion, which was from the beginning very critical of the project. Enormous amounts of public money were being spent, old historical buildings were being torn down, and who knew what would go up?

A basic program for the future building was worked out in June 1970. It contained a definition of objectives, a description of the various activities, functional diagrams and flow-charts of the whole, and the principle spatial characteristics. This program was used as a basis for the international competition. In essence it tried to analyze and articulate the needs of future users without actually prescribing details: each participant in the competition could then express more specifically a personal approach to this set of goals. This so-called "Beaubourg Program" was to help architects avoid the traditional response to a civic building of this sort. Hopefully the architect would seek an original solution, rather than appropriate an existing icon from the architectural past.

The Winning Project

Based on the program guidelines and objectives, an international architectural competition was held early in 1971. An international jury composed of distinguished architects, engineers and museum curators was formed to judge the submitted proposals. Its members were:

M. Jean Prouvé, President (architect, France)
M. Gaétan Picon (former director-general of Arts & Letters, France)
M. Emile Aillaud (architect, France)
Sir Frank Francis (honorary director of the British Museum, England)
Mr. Philip Johnson (architect, United States)
M. Michel Laclotte (chief curator of the Department of Painting at the Louvre)
M. Oscar Niemeyer (architect, Brazil)
M. William Sandberg (former director of the Stedelijk Museum of Amsterdam, Holland)
M. Herman Liebaers (director of the Royal Library of Belgium, Belgium)
M. Henri-Pierre Maillard (architect, France)

681 projects were submitted to the jury, 186 from France and from 49 other countries. The one

which attracted the most attention has some unique features: it occupied only half of the given site, it conformed closely to the program guidelines, and it was, in concept, strikingly simple. Eight out of nine jury members voted for it. The winning project had been submitted by a team of architects: Renzo Piano (Italy) and Richard Rogers (England), in association with the English firm Ove Arup and Partners, engineers.

In the words of the architects who conceived the winning design:

The fundamental concept of the building eliminates the traditional façade. By fading away, the envelope helps to realize the prime objective of the Centre which is to disseminate culture. It becomes transparent. Thanks to the escalators suspended from the west façade, like a gangway thrown onto the hull of a ship, visitors may comprehend both the building and the city. The aerial route is a very powerful invitation to discovery and invitation . . . . It is not just an elitist cultural movement made up of a number of watertight compartments but a people's center, a university of the street capable of reflecting the constantly changing needs of its users.

From the very beginning the architects and their designs met with much opposition and verbal assault from the media and the French public, which lasted throughout the five years of the project. Many reacted negatively to so modern a building in the historical center of Paris. Secondly, at the time the winners were chosen, the pavilions of the old Central Markets were being demolished. The building of Centre Beaubourg was to be begun after the Baltard pavilions had been torn down and a new complex, Le Forum de Commerce et de Loisirs, constructed on the site. Some of the

opposition to Centre Pompidou grew out of a confusion between two completely different projects with totally separate goals: one a national center of art and culture, the other a commercial center. This was further complicated by the fact that the architects did not speak French, and they had to work in France under the French system of building. French architects protested and organized a group called "Le Geste Architectural," and tried to stop the project by a series of lawsuits. After many negotiations and a special vote in the National Assembly, Piano and Rogers were given complete control over the project.

The next step was to find a building company in France which could handle a project of such dimensions, and develop a good working relationship with foreign architects and engineers. When Piano and Rogers took over control of the project they also assumed full responsibility for

The approach to Centre Pompidou from Les Halles district to the west. Les Halles is the busiest central transportation node in Paris, bringing millions of visitors from many different metropolitan and regional areas. It is an animated and pleasant district for shopping, strolling, eating and relaxing, but above all for partaking in the Centre's many offerings, most for free. The areas connecting Les Halles and Centre Pompidou have been made into a large pedestrian district, which revives the traditional pleasures of the promenade and the sidewalk cafe.

the project cost: their architectural fee, which included a share for the consultant, was fixed at 12%, but in case of cost increases it would be reduced to 6.7% and if increases exceeded 50%, it would be reduced to a mere 4.6%.

Although some concessions had to be made, the architects were able to realize not only their own dream but the dream of a whole generation of architects, from the Russian Constructivists of the 1920s to the Archigram in England (of which Rogers was a direct product) in the 1960s.

The precursors of the Piano-Rogers design are Constructivists, Futurists, Archigramists, Metabolists. London's Crystal Palace of 1851 is probably the earliest model. Another influential structure was the Constructivist project for the Pravda Building by the Vesnin Brothers in 1921. Like the Vesnin project, the Piano-Rogers design was very similar to an industrial building. In both,

elevators run up and down the façade, and the whole building could be used to display advertising signs or projecting screens. In both, architecture integrated not only the functional elements but also non-architectural elements such as multi-media shows. But the true precursor for this type of building goes back to 1931, when Le Corbusier began to develop the "twentieth century museum concept," known as the square spiral museum. The building could grow according to need, means and resources. In addition to the building itself, Le Corbusier envisioned (and actually planned, in successive drafts for an International Art Center) functions and spaces that figure prominently in the Piano-Rogers design of 1971: music, dance, theater, audio-visual projections, and even provisions for spontaneous happenings in the open air. In 1963, the Culture Ministry under André Malraux proposed to Le Corbusier that he build his twentieth-century museum for the La Défense district of Paris. The project was announced at a press conference that same year, but the project suffered delays, for there had yet been no specific site allocated. And in 1965 came Corbusier's tragic death. Beaubourg, although ultimately designed by foreign architects, became the heir to these unrealized plans of the great master.

Versatility is one of those qualities architects have been striving to achieve for a long time, especially in this sort of building, but it has seldom been realized on such a grand scale and in a structure housing so many disciplines and activities. In order to achieve maximum flexibility and adaptability, all the mechanical services, as well as structural elements, are exposed. It is like a human body with all its organs and systems externalized, including the skeleton. There is something both honest and grotesque about this unmasking.

All these "organic systems" are color coded,

so participants can understand the building's metabolism. The structural skeleton is painted white. All other colors symbolize dynamic services, providing the building with its vital fluids: blue for air, green for water, red for vertical transportation and yellow for electricity. The parts fit together like a giant erector set, giving the impression of an open-ended structure to which one could add pieces, in both directions without effecting its essential existing structure. Each level is made up of a bridge fifty meters long, supported on both sides by columns forty-two meters apart, balanced by a system of flexible arms called gerberettes. The same structural technique is applied to the interior of the building, and to the floors as well, permitting them to be lifted or lowered at will. The building could change totally its interior proportions, its partitions and floor heights.

One of the unique features of the Piano-Rogers design is the vast open space in front of the building, as large as the space occupied by the building itself. This piazza, a slightly sloping public square, serves as a street theatre in which anyone can perform, amuse and amaze. The escalator for major circulation to any level, and long promenade decks running the full length of the building, are placed along the piazza façade, permitting the visitor to participate in the public square's activities and enjoy the panoramic view of Paris beyond.

Ever since the Middle Ages, the squares and streets of Paris have been used as living theatres for spontaneous events, circus acts and entertainment. The new Place Beaubourg is no exception. The architects of the Centre generously allocated as much space for open-air public activities as for the building itself. The gently-sloping plaza, paved with cobblestones, is everyone's stage: a sole acrobat or a fire-eater; a lonely musician or a full orchestra. Place Beaubourg is a historical prototype of a major urban space where crowds can act or interact, where the difference between performer and audience is abolished, and where there is no language barrier. This plaza is part of a larger pedestrian district, connecting Centre Pompidou to the Forum of Les Halles through a network of small neighborhood streets and squares reclaimed for the pedestrian.

"...It is not just an elitist cultural monument made up of a number of watertight compartments but a people's center, a university of the street capable of reflecting the constantly changing needs of its users..." (Piano and Rogers)

Architects & Engineers: Nuts and Bolts

Throughout the development of the Beaubourg Project, from its inception to its completion, there was a close cooperation between the architects, engineers, consultants and contractors. The result was a product of team effort, not of a single individual mind; it is a synthesis of architecture, engineering and technology.

Richard Rogers was born in 1933, and Renzo Piano in 1937; they met in 1969, at exactly the time when Pompidou was considering a National Center of Art & Culture. Rogers graduated from the Architectural Association in London, and received his Master's Degree from Yale's School of Architecture. He practiced in London, and built small office buildings and factories.

Renzo Piano, the son of a building contractor in Genoa, had done some innovative work in lightweight structures before going to England. While in London, doing research on the work of Richard Rogers, Piano met Rogers, and they soon became partners. Work on the competition design took them three months.

The building was to house three major departments (the Music Research Center was not yet incorporated) in a simple, transparent and flexible cage. Its windows were to be screens, displaying information to the outside by television projection run by computers. The architects' primary concern was to design a structure that would be versatile and not specific, capable of adapting kinetically to a real situation, internal or external. In other words, the architectural design was not derived from any preconceived style or form, but from an ever-

changing function. In our age this could only be an "urban machine" and not the more traditional monument. The building was a tool which had to be in principle unfinished so it could be continually modified. In their design the architects specified a metal structure creating vast open spaces piled vertically over five floors. This decision was not questioned and the initial concept, minus the TV projections on inner and outer walls, was realized with no major alteration.

Piano and Roger's preliminary design scheme of 1971 provided for 125,000 m² instead of the prescribed 100,000 m². The cost estimate also

The main escalator, suspended from the structure and enclosed in a transparent tube, runs the full length of the building. Not only does it give visitors access to every floor, but it keeps them in contact with all the happenings down below, in the public square and surrounding areas. The top of the escalator provides a breathtaking panorama of Paris: Notre Dame, Tour St. Jacques, Eiffel Tower and Sacré-Coeur . . . (Photograph on the opposite page by Laurent Rousseau).

rose, and for the first time a budget was mentioned. This design was not accepted, and the architects had to review the design strictly in keeping with the program guidelines.

A second preliminary design was presented in 1972 and the price tag at this time was 265 million French francs; this was accepted by Pompidou. A detailed design was submitted by the consultants in December of 1972, and the price rose to 296 million francs. A more finalized design followed in the spring of 1973; this was to go to different contractors for bids, and the price was now 325 million francs. Since this was a major public building, fire protection precautions were very strict, and these additional measures added another 20 million francs to the project.

Spiraling costs and the dispersing of responsibility for the building led to something of a crisis even before construction had begun. Piano and Rogers had as one of their aesthetic aims for the building the abolition of a rigorous distinction between architecture and interior design. At the outset, the architects were entrusted only with the building superstructure, and the interior landscape, furnishings, partitions and audio-visual equipment were to be handled by others. This conflict was ultimately resolved in favor of the architects; they were even allowed to play a part in decisions affecting the larger urban areas surrounding the complex. This struggle of the architects for autonomy over their own building was a major event, resulting in actual reform of building

Air-conditioning units in white and elevator machine rooms in red are located on the roof. The exposed blue pipes run down the outside of the building, delivering air-conditioning to every level along the façade and ceiling. The color code is consistent, and provides the curious visitor with an instant understanding of the system, an open book to the wonders of architectural language. Passenger and freight elevators are also exposed and painted red. Main-bearing columns, gerberettes and tension rods are painted white, while the main beams are clad in stainless steel sheeting. All the structural and environmental parts of the system were prefabricated and standardized for easy assembly in the field.

procedures for all of France.

Before Centre Pompidou, an architect would submit a sketch, and then another firm would develop a design into a buildable project, after which a contractor would come in and execute the actual building. There was no control, over the evolution of plans or over the costs. When Piano and Rogers realized this procedure, they moved quickly to set up their own office together with Ove Arup in Paris. They fought for the right for an unprecedented type of contract. The architectural team was given total control and supervision of the design, quality, planning and cost liability. If cost increased over a certain percentage, Piano and Rogers would have to take a cut on their commission. Two years after this contract was approved, a general reform in the procedures governing the design of public buildings was passed.

Construction began in 1973. It was necessary that the structure be prefabricted and assembled in a short period of time. While the substructure basement and parking levels underground were being built, the superstructure was being prepared for assembly. The superstructure was in fact up within ten months, a record time for a building of such dimensions. This type of construction needed no welding or any other complex field operations, only the simple putting-together of different pieces of a puzzle. The coordination of the building operation was in the hands of the major French building concern, Grands Travaux de Marseille. The main load-bearing structure was supplied and erected by the German firm Krupp. The steel columns were manufactured in France by Pont-a-Mousson, by pouring liquid steel into rapidly rotating tube molds lined with sand. The outside diameter of the columns is 85 cm, and the thickness of its outside wall varies from 40 to 85 mm. Their height is composed of three sections: the first attached to the foundation is 5 meters high, the second 23 meters, and the third 21 meters high and is welded to the second.

The cast-iron flexible arms, called *gerberettes*, are named after the nineteenth century German bridge-builder Gerber, and were fabricated by Krupp from wooden casts. Each piece is eight meters long and weighs about ten tons. The gerberettes were the most difficult component parts of the structure to manufacture. Once cast, each gerberette had to be thermally treated against easy failure and inspected for any flaw in production and load-tested before being accepted for use. The main beams are made of rolled steel tubes of 419 mm exterior diameter. These tubes are welded into an assembly measuring 48 meters long, 2.5 meters deep and weighing 70 tons.

Prefabricated parts from the many shops were transported by rail and temporarily stored in the

Structural component parts: the round vertical shaft is the column, the horizontal flexible arm is a gerberette—the meeting point of the floor beams and diagonal steel bars for structural stability.

Paris region, and delivered to the job site as needed. Transportation of the heavy prefabricated main beams posed real problems. Special train cars were used, each equipped to carry three beams. Truck trailers delivered these pieces to the site at night. The ten-ton gerberettes were transported directly from Rohrbach to Paris by truck.

In order to eliminate even the smallest risk in construction failure, all the structural components were tested, some by the manufacturers and client representatives, others by independent institutes in Germany, England and France. These included surface crack tests, ultrasonic tests, magnetic particles inspection, tensile and compressive tests, temperature tests, hardness measurements. And the main structural members were tested carrying 120% of their maximum load.

Fire insurance companies imposed strict rules for Centre Pompidou. The architects provided large exterior fire escape stairs, built according to a scissors concept, every second floor is connected to the same staircase, in case of overload. The building also contains irreplaceable value in its art collections. Therefore sophisticated equipment was installed to detect fire and extinguish it immediately. The materials used in the structure, furniture and fittings are fireproof or do not produce toxic fumes upon combustion. To prevent the spread of fire, the building was divided into separate compartments formed by fire walls. Water-filled shutters close automatically, activated by both fire and solar gain. The main load-bearing columns are filled with water which is circulated by pumps and kept below 100 degrees centigrade; this can be used as a reserve in case of fire. The steel structure joints have also been protected from fire by vermiculite based spray, and the beams clad with rock wool shells enclosed in stainless steel sheaths. This gives two-hour fireproofing

Photograph by
Laurent Rousseau

to the entire structure. Even the ducts for heating, ventilating and air conditioning have been designed to withstand fire for two hours. Faults which occur in the system are signalled to the central control room where firefighting personnel are always present. There is also an alarm system on the premises of the Centre's Central Technical Administration connected to a computer system. Twenty-three TV screens are connected to 120 cameras monitoring the floor areas.

To evaluate the success or failure of Centre Pompidou it is necessary to know its history, its purposes, its programming, but especially its design, by which the architects realized the final product. This understanding permits users to draw closer to the experience of those who created it. It is impossible to avoid a confrontation with the architecture or a reaction to its honesty of expression: columns, beams, gerberettes, escalators, elevators, ducts and ventilators, all exposed, composed, entangled, divergent, pure lines against the sky. As we approach it, it comes to life as an object and a symbol. We need not even go inside to get the answers posed by the outside, to penetrate behind the façades. Centre Pompidou is a true paradoxical object; what is inside, and what is outside?

The overall impact of the building, from afar and from close up, is that of a great new mystery, a sort of abstract art, a new urban myth.

The technological side of Centre Pompidou, as seen along the narrow neighboring rue Simon-le-Franc. It is a scene to provoke the shouting President Pompidou, even before the building was constructed: "Ça va faire crier!" Centre Pompidou has since become the most controversial building in Paris. Should such architecture be inserted into an old historical neighborhood, with old stone walls and gabled roofs and delicately-proportioned windows? And yet the building of the Centre has led to the rehabilitation of the entire district. Without Beaubourg, this multicolored intruder and catalyst of change, the entire quarter might have been pulled down. Many new tenants have moved into the district, attracted by its magnetic presence. (Photograph by Laurent Rousseau)

A New Building for a New Culture

Beaubourg was perceived by its architects as an integral part of its surrounding district. It was to serve a large and changing public, for a hundred years or more. This was a different view of museums, and the museum going public. The old rule "form follows function" was not a guideline, because the functions of this new building were to be potentially endless and constantly changing.

One of these functions was to provide general information and exposure to modern art to an indiscriminate public. The first French museums were built by and for the elite. The Louvre, which opened in 1793, did not admit the general public, and was open to artists only five out of ten days. In the nineteenth century, museums became truly public and grew greatly in popularity, but in these museums the type of art displayed was largely traditional and the buildings in which it was displayed were very conservative. Beaubourg was to be the first cultural institution in France devoted entirely to modern art, and to the new mass culture. It was conceived not only as a place for displaying art, but also as a radical place where the artist could come into direct contact with the public. The public could seek the help and advice of experts in problems arising from their everyday life and immediate environment. Art was not only something to look at, but something to participate in.

The most important aspect of this action was to develop the feelings and appetites of individuals toward modern art and culture. This was not a traditional view of art in France, which was one reason why the building has aroused so much enthusiasm, criticism and hostility. During the early years, President Pompidou was inspiring support for the project. His goal was to bridge the gap between the general public and those who actually produced art or devised technology. Despite the cost of the Centre, Pompidou felt that Beaubourg was an extremely small portion of the total funds spent for culture in the National Budget. In April of 1974, Pompidou died. His successor, Valéry Giscard d'Estaing, only had a little interest in modern art and was committed to a reduction in government spending. He stopped two major projects underway: the Left Bank Expressway planned under Pompidou, and the Les Halles Commercial project. Giscard d'Estaing also tried to reduce the size of Beaubourg by cutting one floor and enclosing the open side of the building. Mme. Pompidou informed the president how dear to the heart of the late president the Beaubourg project had been, and the architects informed him that since the floors came in pairs, it would be quite impossible to cut only one. The project remained intact, and was renamed by official governmental decree "Centre National d'Art et de Culture Georges Pompidou." Problems still remained. In 1975, attacks were launched in the National Assembly and the Senate, accusing the builders of destroying historical Paris, using non-French architects, consuming funds that could be better spent elsewhere. Some cuts were made and some cancellations, but at this point most of the material was already on the site and cutting would have been more costly than construction. At first some refused to let their collections be moved to Beaubourg, on the grounds that the works might be badly displayed or perhaps not displayed at all. After long negotiations, most of the works were moved into the new building. The building opened to the public on February 2, 1977.

Photograph on the next page by Laurent Rousseau

A Guide to the Facilities

Anyone can enter: art amateurs, book lovers, cinema lovers, anyone desiring to find out what this cultural machine has to offer. No one is forced to follow protocol. Everyone can flip through the mass of newspapers, journals and books, listen to the latest releases in music, watch a special program on television, have a drink or a cup of coffee. And everyone is free to talk to his neighbor or remain absorbed and indifferent. It is quite a change from the traditional operation of libraries and museums.

The building has two underground levels for parking under the plaza, a ground level with mezzanine, and five floors above.

Ground Floor (entering from the plaza side)

This level is referred to as the *Forum*, and it functions more or less as its historical Roman prototype. This is a mixing chamber for all who enter and exit, and is worth observing before proceeding upward. Here the visitor can stop to ask for information or to pick up the weekly program

showing day by day activities in all the different departments, can arrange for a special guided tour entitled "La Découverte du Centre," offered daily and limited to twenty-five people.

In the middle of the Forum, emerging from a sunken space, there is a major display area featuring the main exhibit of the day: an offshore drilling platform, or a huge theatre curtain designed by Picasso, or for the Dali exhibit, a Citroen taxi suspended from the ceiling over a teaspoon.

To the right of the entry is the access to the Children's Workshop (Atelier des Enfants). There are also two contemporary galleries on the ground floor, featuring young artists and photographers. This space was provided because of pressure from the younger generation of French artists, who did not wish to be excluded from the Centre. Below the mezzanine and behind the sunken space is a book shop; one of the best equipped in Paris in the fields of art, architecture, and art catalogues. To the left of the entry, over the escalator, there is a large Vasarély portrait of President Pompidou, a computer-generated, three-dimensional image made from metal strips.

Directly beyond the escalator is a *News Room* (Salle de'Actualité) with the latest newspapers, journals and reviews in French and many foreign languages. It is provided with a lecture space where writers may present their latest work to the public. At one side of the room, recording jackets are arranged by composer and type; a visitor can hear any recording by taking a jacket to the attendant, who then provides a chair and earphones, all for free. If all ten record players are occupied, anyone can be plugged into another's music; currently playing titles are posted. Casette tapes of the recent productions from the Centre's own Music Research Center are also available, and some of these can be purchased. Here one can consult a portfolio containing all the activities

The Children's Workshop is reserved for children ages 4 to 12 only, where they express their creative impulses without adult interference. Finger and brush painting on an enamelled wall are among the many tools made available.

41

of the Centre and neighboring provinces, with reviews (Dossier de Presse). There is also a Suggestion Book (Cahier de Suggestions). Every entry is answered, either in the book or with a personal letter, so write legibly and leave your address!

The *Information-Reference Library of the Industrial Design Center* (Documentation-Information du CCI) is located behind the poster, books and card stand. It contains all the newest releases purchased by the Centre's Library, and an impressive reference library on the subjects of art, architecture, urban planning and industrial design. Portfolios on these subjects are so well arranged and up to date that this small library is full of students doing their homework assignments.

To the right of the escalator is a display pavilion devoted to the cultural activities of the provinces, *Crossroads of the Regions* (Carrefour des Régions). Short-circuit TV screens project programs from the regional centers, and exhibitions from the Centre are loaned and exchanged.

Thus the sections assembled on the Forum level represent, in miniature, all the major activities of the Centre: library, music, visual art, modern technology, dissemination of information.

The Children's Workshop (L'Atelier des Enfants) occupies the right wing off the forum, in full view of the plaza and all its activities. The architect who designed it collaborated closely with his clients, children. In the Children's Art Room, those between four and twelve are initiated into the plastic arts, audio-visual appreciation and body movement. Special provisions are made for the handicapped. No adults other than the specially-trained educators are permitted.

The goal of the Workshop is to expose very young children to contemporary education in the arts, of the sort that is not yet readily available in the schools. A *Creativity Studio* develops the senses of hearing, taste and smell. The *Recreation Workshop* focuses on speaking, moving, dancing, and mime using puppets, masks and make-up. Teachers from Parisian and provincial schools are invited to the Workshop for initiation into the pedagogy of artistic expression, which they can then apply in their own classrooms. There is also a lending service, through which the Workshop sends a variety of pre-packaged materials and exhibits to the provinces for a month at a time: "Art & Technique," "Art & Nature," "Shelter & Environment," and other similar topics.

To avoid turning this Children's Center into the capital's most popular nursery, a child must be enrolled one week in advance in writing, usually as a member of a particular group or school.

Across the plaza in the left wing off the Forum is the *Children's Library* (Bibliothèque des Enfants). It is built to size and scale for those between the ages of six and twelve, and adults are not admitted.

The Children's Library is reserved exclusively for those between the ages of 6 and 12, who can enter directly from the east side of the plaza. The glazed wall panes keep the children in constant visual contact with the activities outside on the square. Inside the library the emphasis is upon an awakening in the young person of a taste for the marvelous world of the written word, the image, and the imagination. Furniture is designed to the scale of its clients. (Photograph by Laurent Rousseau)

Mezzanine (street level from Rue du Renard and secondary entry to the Centre)

The *Gallery of Retrospective Art* (Galerie rétrospective) exhibits objects and documents showing the evolution of industrial age civilization in the nineteenth and twentieth centuries. A twenty-minute audio-visual projection is continually running, to complement the wall images, and shows inventions and methods up to the Great Universal Exhibition of 1851 in London.

The *Current Events Gallery of the CCI* (Galerie d'Actualité du CCI) is a space permanently reserved for changing exhibits such as architecture, and the problems individuals face in dealing with their surroundings.

The *Contemporary Galleries (Galeries contemporaires)* are a part of the National Museum of Modern Art, and similar in purpose to the two on the ground floor. It features one-person shows or group exhibits of major contemporary artists, French and foreign.

First Floor

The only public facility on this floor is the huge *Public Information Library* (BPI, or Bibliothèque Publique D'Information), entered from the floor above. Access to the library is free, and the reader can consult any book, periodical, slide, map or microfilm from open stacks. Professional help is available, there are no forms to fill out; everyone helps themselves. No material can be removed from the premises. The library accomodates 1,300 visitors on the chairs and tables, and many more on the carpet. Approximately 10,000 visit daily. In spite of these large numbers, the library is generally a calm place. The language laboratory is also located here.

The remaining part of this floor is occupied by administrative offices of the Centre, and public entry is not allowed.

Second Floor

The Public Library entrance is from this level, and from here one circulates to its upper and lower sections. The visitor is greeted by a librarian (one of many dispersed throughout the library) who explains the library and its classification system. There are three catalogues and a computer which can provide an entire bibliography on any subject. The librarians are multilingual and very helpful. A projection room, *Salle Jean Renoir*, is available for movies and videotape projections.

Third Floor

The only entry to the *National Museum of Modern Art*, Musée National d'Art Moderne (MNAM) is from this floor, although the MNAM's permanent collection occupies the entire fourth floor. There are three different sections of the Museum at this level:

1. *Drawings, Photographs and Prints.* It is reserved for changing exhibits and is usually free of charge.

2. *Kandinsky Salon.* It is straight ahead from the main entry and serves as a passageway into the museum collections. The Salon is a reconstruction from Kandinsky's sketches of his 1922 "Salon de Musique."

3. *Permanent collections of the MNAM.* This collection features artists from the beginning of the twentieth century, and includes paintings, sculpture, etchings, drawings and photographs. It is arranged chronologically and displayed on walls, partitions and movable panels.

The major movements of the early part of the twentieth century are represented here:

Fauvism (Derain, Dufy, Matisse, Vlaminck)
Cubism (Braque, Gris, Picasso)
Italian Futurism
Russian Avant-garde (Gontcharova, Larionov, Pougny)

Photograph on the preceding two pages by Laurent Rousseau

Beginning of the Abstract (Robert and Sonia
    Delaunay, Kandinsky, Kupka)
There is a section of 800 works stored within the
gallery but suspended overhead which can be
lowered and viewed by any visitor.

On this floor also is a cinéma (Le Cinéma du
Musée) used for the projection of films, docu-
mentaries, experimental movies and video. The
program and presentation of these is usually
related to the exhibits of the museum.

Fourth floor

The access to this floor is an interior escalator
from the entry level below. It is entirely occupied
by MNAM, which in addition to painting and
indoor sculpture, includes three exterior sculpture
terrace gardens.

Here the major movements of twentieth century art continue, beginning at the head of the
escalator with a sequence of four Matisse Backs.
Then, proceeding through the museum:

Picasso 1920–1940
Braque after 1920
Cubism after 1918
Purism & abstract art with Mondrian and
    Pevsner, 1920–1940
Russian avant garde with Malevich after 1917
Klee 1920s
Dada
Arp
Hausmann
Picabia
Kandinsky of Bauhaus and Paris, 1922–1944
Matisse & Léger after 1920
Chagall
Bonnard
The Painters of Montparnasse:
    Modigliani, Soutine
Naif painters
European Expressionists after Fauvism:

Derain, Dufy, Marquet 1920–1940
Dada & Surrealism:
    Dali, Ernst, Miró 1920–1945
Confrontations 1945: Picasso & Gonzales

The three outdoor terraces are on the north,
south, and west sides. For security reasons these
terraces are rarely open to the public, but they
can be viewed from several vantage points on the
upper floor.

The north end contains exhibitions of contemporary art, whose themes are constantly
changing to incorporate the most recent in artistic
achievement. Among its exhibits have been: The
Art of the 1950s, The Lyric Abstraction, The Cobra
Group, The New Realism, Abstract Art in the USA
after 1945, Geometrical Abstractions after 1945,
Op, Pop, and Kinetic Art, The Art of the Sixties,
the Seventies, and Super-realism.

The point of departure for the MNAM's collection is considered to be the Fauvist movement
circa 1905, with its major representatives Matisse,
Derain and Van Dongen. The collection has its
origin in the old Museum of Modern Art holdings,

47

but many new paintings were acquired by the Centre. They include German expressionists, abstracts, pop artists, and the American artists Pollock, Rothko, Newman, Lichtenstein, Motherwell, Noland and Warhol.

Visitors can find in each section information sheets on particular paintings or artists. Every afternoon a museum expert offers a twenty-minute lecture on a painting or artist. In the MNAM, traditional uniformed guards have been replaced by hosts and hostesses always willing to help and inform the visitors.

For the general public or serious scholars, the Museum also offers free of charge the services of an information center and library, containing catalogues, archives, and several thousand portfolios of contemporary artists.

Fifth floor

The fifth and top floor contains the following services in order of their proximity to the end of the escalator: bar and restaurant with an outdoor terrace, Cinémathèque Française, Changing Exhibits space for major theme shows. There is also a panoramic view of Paris and a fine view of the open sculpture terraces of the Museum on the floor below.

There is also a Restaurant Panoramique, "Le Toit des Arts," with table service and prix fixe dinners. The busy little bar is located at the entry and serves mostly coffee, soft drinks and beer. There is a sign announcing "Picnic interdit," meaning, do not bring your own food and eat it here.

The *Cinématèque* auditorium is specially equipped for movies of the French Cinema Archives, founded by Henri Langlois, and shows masterpieces of film history as well as festivals of avant garde filmmakers around the world. There are three or four showings a day. The Cinémathèque is not an ordinary commercial theatre; it is an extension of the old Cinémathèque Française in Palais de Chaillot.

The remaining part of this floor is a flexible loft space used for temporary exhibits. They may, depending on their theme, be organized by any of the four major departments. These exhibits, individual or collective, are based on an important contemporary theme or problem, such as the recent series on the contributions to art made by various world capitals: Paris-New York, Paris-Berlin, Paris-Moscow, Paris-Paris.

The three underground levels

Tours of the Centre begin on the *first underground level,* around a great architectural model of Centre Pompidou. To the right are two auditoriums devoted to theatre and dance, Grande Salle and Petite Salle, flexible performance areas permitting various forms of stage settings. It is the Centre's policy to give young writers, dramatists and choreographers a chance to perform their works here. The first dance workshops were offered in 1979. The Centre intends to host different experimental dance demonstrations which could be performed not only on the stage in a classical tradition, but also choreographed and presented to the public around a particular painting or sculpture piece, elsewhere in the Centre's highly flexible space.

Below the Forum (*second underground level*) the substructure contains technical and storage areas such as computer, photographic security control and mechanical services. Under the square is a parking area for cars.

The *third underground level* contains services only: ventilation, heating and cooling plant, art storage rooms, janitorial offices and television studios.

In the *fourth underground level,* only a partial floor, are located the water reserves, cooling pumps and drainage.

The outdoor café at the top of the building, with a panoramic view over Paris: Hôtel-de-Ville, Notre-Dame Cathedral, Panthéon, and the Left Bank beyond. During the summer months, the interior café on the 5th floor expands onto this outdoor terrace, giving visitors the opportunity to relax in the open air and absorb the visual stimuli, art, and architecture surrounding them on all sides.

The Brancusi Workshop
(L'Atelier Brancusi)

It is a separate structure situated outside the Centre proper in its own building. Constantin Brancusi was born in Rumania in 1876 and lived in Paris from 1904 until his death in 1957. He worked marble, metal and wood into abstract forms. In 1956 he became a French citizen, and donated his entire studio to the French government. The *Brancusi Workshop* is a faithful reconstruction of the artist's studio at No. 11 Impasse Ronsin, which has been torn down. A partial reconstruction was made in 1961 and housed in the old Museum of Modern Art; this new reconstruction is now part of the National Museum.

Interior views of the famous artist's studio, reconstructed here for the National Museum of Modern Art. From 1916 until his death, Constantin Brancusi lived and worked in this modest atelier, attracting many other artists around him. Here his tools as well as many of his sculptures are displayed at different stages of their completion, and in different materials—bronze, wood, stone, and plaster. He was always striving for perfection, meticulously caring for each detail, and reducing the form to its purest abstraction: some examples shown here include the Fish, the Seal, the Bird in space, the Kiss, torsos and endless columns. (Photograph above by Laurent Rousseau)

The National Museum of Modern Art is located on the third and fourth floors. The west façade of the fourth floor has an outdoor sculpture terrace, where many of the masterpieces are displayed in open air and natural lighting. The window shutters can be operated manually to control the quality of the light inside the galleries, to dramatize a particular work on display or to open completely and make the outdoor areas part of the interior. (Photograph by Laurent Rousseau)

Administration	1st floor
Bar	5th floor
Book Shop	Forum level (under Mezzanine)
Brancusi Workshop	Piazza level (off Rue St. Martin)
Cafeteria	5th floor
Changing exhibits (Grande Galerie)	5th floor
Children's Library	Piazza (north)
Children's Workshop	Piazza (south)
Cinéma of the Museum (MNAM)	3rd floor
Cinémathèque	5th floor
Contemporary Galleries	Ground floor & Mezzanine
Crossroads of the Regions	Forum level
Current Events Gallery (CCI)	Mezzanine
Drawings & Prints (MNAM)	3rd floor
Gallery of Retrospective Art (CCI)	Mezzanine
Grande Salle	First Underground level
Guided Tours	Ground Floor
Industrial Age Design Center (CCI)	Mezzanine
Information-Reference Library (CCI)	Forum level
Kandinsky Salon (MNAM)	3rd floor
Language Laboratory (BPI)	1st floor (enter from 2nd)
Library, Public Information (BPI)	2nd floor
Music Research Center (IRCAM)	Place Igor Stravinsky
Museum of Modern Art (MNAM)	3rd floor
News Room (BPI)	Forum level
Petite Salle	First Underground level
Photography (MNAM)	3rd floor
Prints (MNAM)	3rd floor
Reception	Ground Floor (Piazza side)
Restaurant	5th floor
Salle Jean Renoir	2nd floor

Centre Pompidou is open 12 noon to 10 p.m. every day except Tuesday.
Saturday, Sunday and holidays, 10 a.m. to 10 p.m.

Information (telephone) 277-1233
Programs (telephone) 277-1112

The Four Main Departments

The four main departments of the Centre—
the Museum, the Library, the Industrial Age Design Center and the Music Research Center—are
very diverse, but all are similar in one way: each
represents, for France, a new approach to a cultural facility. This chapter will consider these
approaches in historical context, their development and ultimate embodiment in Centre
Pompidou.

1. Le Musée National d'Art Moderne

(MNAM) [The National Museum of Modern Art]
The National Museum of Modern Art is the
culmination of many years' progress in the domain
of modern art in France. Its beginnings were in
the 19th century, under Napoleon III, when the
"Salon des Refusés" [The Salon of the Rejected]
was founded for creative artists who had been
rejected by the Salon of the Royal Academy. It

was later renamed "Salon des Artistes Indépendants." Any artist was given the opportunity to exhibit up to three works of art once a year. Although often ridiculed, the "Indépendants" were the true founders of the modern art movement in France.

The famous poet Charles Baudelaire was a frequent critic and reviewer of many exhibitions held at different salons between 1845 and 1862. He considered Delacroix "the most original painter of modern times," and he called Daumier a draftsman of genius; Ingres was proclaimed better than both of them in drawing and painting. Baudelaire was instrumental in acquainting the French public with its own modern artists and their work. The Universal Exhibition of 1855 added vitality to the movement by exposing the public to the work of foreign artists as well.

In the second half of the 19th century, arts such as painting, etching and sculpture were joined by photography as a new artistic medium —although it was not recognized as such until much later. Daguerre perfected his new technique in 1837 and then took specific steps to ensure that photography would become a popular artform, available to all. He wrote an instructional booklet with scale drawings of the camera and equipment as well as simplified directions for its use by the general public. Enthusiasm spread, and France consequently produced generations of great professional photographers, masters at art, action and documentary: Le Secq, Nadar, Atget, Nègre, Latrigue, Cartier-Bresson. Centre Pompidou recognizes photography as one of the great modern arts and incorporates it into its collections.

In the 20th century, the most direct precursor of the Museum of Modern Art was the annual exhibition, "Salon d'Automne." It was founded in 1903 by an association of artists which originally included Rodin and the Fauves group. Yearly exhibits were held at the Grand Palais, and a jury would grant prizes for selected works. Gaugin's

The "Paris-Paris" exhibit during 1981, which retraced the artistic movements and achievements in Paris during the twenty years between 1937 and 1957. The exhibit featured the prototype of a 2 hp Citroën with one single headlight, among the paintings, sculptures, architecture, literature and decor and design of the period. The National Museum of Modern Art contains 15,000 paintings, sculpture and other works representing modern art since 1905, beginning with Fauvism. Arranged chronologically over the third and fourth level, they cover an area close to 10,000 m², a flexible and adjustable space with no columns or bearing walls.

reputation was established by a memorial exhibition of his work at the first Salon; other major exhibitions which followed included Cezanne, Utrillo, Picabia, Modigliani, El Greco, as well as Fauves and Cubists.

Gradually progress was made in finding a permanent home for exhibiting the masterpieces of modern art. In 1922, a museum for contemporary foreign artists was formed at the Jeu de Paume. In 1937 there were plans to locate a national museum of modern art along with the Museum for the City of Paris in Palais de Tokyo, on the Avenue du President Wilson. Only a portion of the museum was actually open at the time of the 1937 Exhibition, and the remainder had to wait ten years for completion, after many setbacks including the Second World War. The conditions for exhibiting art there were less than ideal: lighting conditions were poor, the roof leaked, and air conditioning often broke down. Funds were also chronically insufficient to maintain it. However, the museum acquired a sizable collection of some well-known artists of the ''School of Paris.''

In 1959, André Malraux, de Gaulle's Minister of Cultural Affairs, organized ''Paris Biennale'' at the Museum of Modern Art. It was a return to the concept of the salon, and specifically for young artists under the age of 35. Malraux chose Le Corbusier, at this time enjoying prominence as the greatest living architect, to draw up plans for a Museum of Modern Art projected for the La Défense district in the early 1960s. But Le Corbusier died in 1965, and his long search for a new type of museum, a ''museum of unlimited growth'', was not realized in Paris. In 1969 de Gaulle's successor, Georges Pompidou, decided to incorporate the latest museum of modern art into a new National Center of Art and Culture planned for Plateau Beaubourg.

Photograph at lower right by Laurent Rousseau

The museum in the Centre thus represents more than a hundred years of evolution, from the salon of the Academy, through the Salon d'Indépendants, the Salon d'Automne, and the modern collections in Jeu de Paume and Palais de Tokyo.

Most of the collections in the old Museum of Modern Art were transferred to the new facility in 1977, with few exceptions, when the owners felt a strong allegiance to the old museum. They resisted transferring their artworks to such a daring building where they might not be displayed to full advantage.

2. La Bibliothèque Publique d'Information
(BPI) [The Public Information Library]

French libraries, like French museums, were generally conceived as institutions for the elite. In 1720 the "Bibliothèque du Roi" opened on the present-day site of the "Bibliothèque Nationale," but it was open only to scholars, under the auspices of his Majesty the King. In the nineteenth century France saw its first municipal, university, and specialized libraries; in 1844-50, a library for students, "Bibliothèque Ste-Geneviève," was built in Paris. The first major project for a limited-access public library did not come until 1868, when such a facility was planned as part of the "Bibliothèque Impériale" (Nationale), then under construction. Public access was limited to one room, Lecture Room B, which closed down in 1935.

Some progress was achieved after 1918 within the various wards of Paris, by the creation of small reading rooms where one could borrow a limited number of books. The quality of the books in their holdings was random and rather poor. In 1963, the Director of Libraries and Reading Rooms undertook to provide new facilities in the district of Les Halles, as part of its renewal and rehabilitation after the Central Markets were torn down. The planned library project was curtailed in 1967 by the Ministry of National Education, and a new location proposed for Plateau Beaubourg. In December 1969, President Pompidou proposed

incorporating a free public library in the new national culture center, alongside the museum. This was officially approved in 1972, the year that construction began on the National Centre.

The new facility within the Centre is a public service information library, open to all, with direct access to its entire collection. It contains several different spaces. On the ground floor, *La Salle d'Actualité* (News Room) makes available newspapers, magazines, music recordings and the lat-

A most successful facility within the complex is the well-equipped library. In addition to an immense collection of books and visual aids, the library offers laboratories for learning languages. (Photograph by Laurent Rousseau)

est releases in books. The Children's Library off the plaza level offers six to twelve year-olds access to books and audiovisual material. The Main Library covers the first, second and third floors, and can seat 1,300 people—three times the capacity of the entire "Bibliothèque Nationale." The first floor contains material on the arts, sports recreation, religion, philosophy, languages and literatures (including a language laboratory); the second floor is general reference and an audiovisual library; the third floor houses the sciences, history, geography and maps.

The acquisitions policy aims at preserving an equal balance between written and audiovisual materials, and between reading material in French and in foreign languages. This rather remarkable policy is a tribute both to the cosmopolitan and international essence of the Centre, and to the more recent recognition that learning is no longer dependent primarily on the printed page.

The library personnel devotes one-third of its work time to welcoming groups and individuals

and acquainting them with the resources. Sophisticated magnetic equipment protects books from illegal removal. The BPI is an enormously rich resource, but it does not permit the circulation of its collection for home use.

Thanks to its flexible architecture and its spirit of innovation, the library can continue to rearrange existing spaces as new patterns of use emerge and the collection expands.

3. Centre de Creation Industrielle
(CCI) [The Industrial Age Design Center]

Decorative arts in France have a long and very rich history. French taste and genius in furniture, tapistry, ceramics, metalwork and interior design have served as the standard in Europe for many centuries, and even today Versailles is unsurpassed as a model of elegance. The development of the decorative arts in France has always been marked by a close cooperation between the patrons of art and the craftsmen or artists. In furniture and architecture, styles are even classified by the names of monarchs or regimes: Louis XIV, Louis

Photographs at lower left and above
by Laurent Rousseau

XV, Louis XVI, Empire, all quite distinct styles. Royal ministers sponsored manufacturing and hired goldsmiths and sculptors to work for the crown.

In more recent times, the definition of "decorative arts" has expanded to include the concepts of architecture, city planning, and the products of modern industry. Le Corbusier was among the first to synthesize all these aspects. In 1924 he wrote an important polemical work entitled "L'Art Decoratif d'Aujourd'hui," calling for a new direction in decorative arts, which had by then become degraded imitations of their great classical prototypes. He devised the radical "Plan Voisin" for urban renewal in the center of Paris, on the occasion of the 1925 International Exhibition of Decorative Arts in Paris. For that exhibition he also built his revolutionary "Pavilion d'Esprit Nouveau," a building so daring that the Exhibition Committee erected a seven-meter high fence around the whole structure so visitors would be spared the sight. The International Jury, however, voted to award Le Corbusier the Exhibition's "Diplôme d'honneur." The President of the jury opposed it, saying, "This is not architecture."

The incorporation of the "Centre de Creation Industrielle" within Centre Pompidou is an extension of this long history of interaction between officials of the government and the new emerging industry and building techniques. A new aesthetic had to be found. CCI, heir to the Central Union of Decorative Arts which itself was the result of a fusion of the Central Union of Beaux Art and the Society of the Museum of Decorative Arts, was created in 1969. It was located in the Marsan Pavilion in the Louvre. It remained there until 1972, when it was integrated into the "Etablissement Public du Centre Beaubourg" and became one of the four major departments in January 1972.

Although the smallest of the four major departments within Beaubourg, the Industrial Age Design Center is one of the most innovative. It is the result of a new aesthetic consciousness: the consideration of contemporary industrial creation from the point of view of its economy as well as its aesthetic and social implications. CCI is the most interdisciplinary of the departments. It focuses on daily life as it is experienced, through objects, tools and architecture. By presenting to the public better-designed products—from coffee grinders to plans for a new city—CCI fosters a new and more enlightened consumerism. The public is given a chance to meet and interact with industrial designers and decision-makers. Services also include exhibitions of general interest on problems of everyday life, publications (books, pamphlets and catalogues), slideshows on various aspects of industrial and interior design and architecture. CCI thus reflects the new spirit and the new times.

CCI is quite different from the museums. It concentrates on ordinary, daily reality rather than high art, trying to make people aware of the aesthetic side of life without forgetting its practical applications. Its emphasis is on the total man-made environment, which we so often poorly understand. It encourages active participation in this environment through a use and appreciation of the most recent technology, thus breaking down the barriers between consumer and producer.

4. Institut de Recherche et Coordination Acoustique/Musique
(IRCAM) [The Music Research Center]

Although the first experiments in serious musical composition using electronic synthesizers and computers began in the 1950s, the idea for IRCAM dates from early 1972. A group of French musicians made a plea for a research cen-

CCI (The Industrial Age Design Center) is not a museum but a multidisciplinary center which seeks to develop in the general public an awareness and sensitivity to the everyday environment. It includes information on architecture, urban planning, industrial design, graphic design, advertising, visual communication, and a multitude of other aspects of ordinary life. CCI sponsors conferences between professionals and for the general public, organizes exhibits, publishes books and information pamphlets, and tries to reach a large audience. This energetic and innovative department continues to grow and expand its services, not only in Paris but throughout France and Europe. ''Galerie retrospective'' offers an audio-visual presentation 20 minutes long, and a permanent wall of images at street level, including documents illustrating the industrial evolution and revolution of the 19th and 20th centuries. (Photograph courtesy of Centre Pompidou)

ter for contemporary music, and President Pompidou decided to include such a center in the new complex at Beaubourg.

The real history and moving force behind IRCAM's project is a single name; Pierre Boulez. Born in France in 1925, he was invited home to head IRCAM after he had been in exile for twenty years, building a musical career in Germany, England and the United States. He left the U.S. in 1977, after six years of conducting the New York Philharmonic, and brought to France fame and originality in the field of contemporary music.

Boulez's return corresponded with the official opening of Centre Pompidou. IRCAM was the embodiment of his dreams, built not only with his consultation but to his specifications. He was also granted autonomy and government subsidies on a scale unknown to the conservatories, universities and radio networks. In return, he was to collaborate with other major institutions of a similar kind in France and abroad. The Music Research Center was the last department to be associated

''Cafés, bistros, et compagnie,'' one of the many exhibits organized by the CCI and sent travelling throughout France, explores the social role played by the café over the last 150 years. (Photograph by Kossa Kowski, courtesy of Centre Pompidou)

Photograph by Laurent Rousseau

with the Centre, opening officially in 1977. It has its own separate budget, its own board of directors, its own separate building. Boulez himself often refers to it as "le petit Beaubourg."

In addition to equipment and facilities, Boulez requested the cooperation of many scientists, acoustic engineers, and computer experts in an effort to consolidate the forces of the musical avant-garde. IRCAM brought together such artists as Vinko Globokar, Luciano Berio, Diego Masson and Iannis Xenakis, among many others. Recently Guiseppe di Giugno, a nuclear physicist and computer expert, joined Boulez, bringing the "4X" computer that he built to assist Boulez in his music research. Boulez is convinced that contemporary technology must become an integral part of modern musical invention, and his goal is a common language between scientists, technicians, and musicians. By the use of computers and synthesizers, IRCAM is involved in the development of a new vocabulary and grammar of music.

IRCAM has at its disposal 3,000 square meters of studios, laboratories, workshops, computer rooms, projection spaces, offices, and a library and reception area, all located underground alongside the main building and below the newly-constructed Plaza Igor Stravinsky. The public can come to the outer reaches of this "secret underground bunker" only on special occasions and with special permission, for the occasional open performance. The principle reason for this isolation is the absolute need for soundproofing, and for a conducive atmosphere for the experts to work undisturbed. The concert hall, 25 meters long, 27 meters wide and 14 meters high, is an instrument in itself, and can be manipulated for the desired configuration in acoustics, instrumentation and seating.

IRCAM is a world apart, but even so it performs social, educational, and public services. Special visits for small groups are scheduled once a week, primarily for musicians and educators, and include an audiovisual presentation, a tour of the workshops, and occasionally a direct musical demonstration. Since computer music, techniques and languages are not taught in most music schools, each year IRCAM invites fifteen to twenty in-residence researchers to use its laboratories. Some applicants are fully funded; others are merely given access to facilities. In addition, courses are offered by a team of one director and four tutors, with a background in both music and computer science. The sessions last six weeks, and can be supplemented by individual courses of study adapted to specific projects.

IRCAM also participates in a large number of presentations organized within the Centre. Every year it offers a series of concerts and workshops in France and abroad, in close collaboration with the "Ensemble Intercontemporain." It produces records, tapes, films, and TV programs.

One of Boulez's recent compositions is entitled "Répons," a 40-minute piece of music using a mixture of natural sounds and sounds transformed by computer. Music critics have called it "radiant and blooming, a great work." Thus twentieth-century music is joining the other innovative departments of Centre Pompidou, returning to France the prestige and leadership in this area which has long been hers.

Photograph below by Nori Okabe

Directions and Statistics

Centre Beaubourg, or simply "Beaubourg," is all you need say to any Parisian, and you will be directed to Centre Georges Pompidou.

However, if you are standing in front of Notre-Dame Cathedral, walk straight north across Pont d'Arcole, a bridge spanning the River Seine and connecting l'Ile de la Cité to the Right Bank. Bypass l'Hôtel-de-Ville and walk three blocks up Rue du Renard. The colorful pipes of the Centre will greet you.

If you are tired of the old masters and leaving the Louvre, walk east along Rue de Rivoli toward Tour St. Jacques, and then turn left on Rue St. Martin. Walk three blocks, and you will be greeted by thousands of people as you arrive on the Plateau Beaubourg.

The best way to establish contact with the Centre is from this plaza side, where an enclosed glass escalator runs the full length and height of the building. Cross the square and enter the Forum, the mixing chamber and heart of the Centre, where you can obtain all the information on different activities.

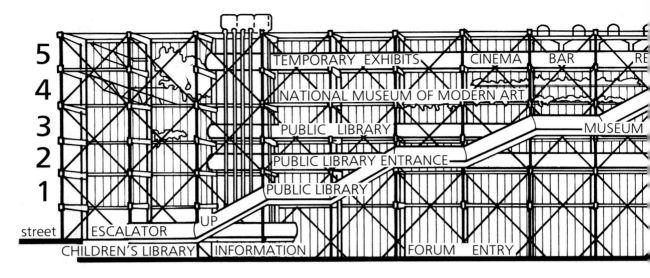

The diagram shows floor levels 5, 4, 3, 2, 1, street, with:
- TEMPORARY EXHIBITS, CINEMA, BAR, RE...
- NATIONAL MUSEUM OF MODERN ART
- PUBLIC LIBRARY, MUSEUM
- PUBLIC LIBRARY ENTRANCE
- PUBLIC LIBRARY
- ESCALATOR, UP
- CHILDREN'S LIBRARY, INFORMATION, FORUM ENTRY

Administration	. . .	1st floor
Bar	. . .	5th Floor
Book Shop	. . . (under Mezzanine)	Forum level
Brancusi Workshop	(off Rue St. Martin)	Piazza level
Cafeteria	. . .	5th floor
Changing Exhibits (Grande Galerie)	. . .	5th floor
Children's Library	. . .	Piazza (north)
Children's Workshop	. . .	Piazza (south)
Cinema of the Museum (MNAM)	. . .	3rd floor
Cinémathèque	. . .	5th floor
Contemporary Galleries	Mezzanine &	Ground floor
Crossroads of the Regions	. . .	Forum
Current Events Gallery (CCI)	. . .	Mezzanine
Drawings & Prints (MNAM)	. . .	3rd floor
Gallery of Retrospective Art (CCI)	. . .	Mezzanine
Grande Salle	. . .	First underground level
Guided Tours	. . .	Ground floor
Industrial Age Design Center (CCI)	. . .	Mezzanine
Information-Reference Library (CCI)	. . .	Forum level
Kandinsky Salon (MNAM)	. . .	3rd floor
Language Laboratory (BPI)	.1st floor, entry from 2nd
Library, Public Information (BPI)	. . .	2nd floor
Music Research Center (IRCAM)	. .	Place Igor Stravinsky
Museum of Modern Art (MNAM)	. . .	3rd floor
News Room (BPI)	. . .	Forum level
Petite Salle	. . .	First underground level
Photography (MNAM)	. . .	3rd floor
Prints (MNAM)	. . .	3rd floor
Reception	. . .	Ground floor, piazza side
Restaurant	. . .	5th floor
Salle Jean Renoir	. . .	2nd floor

Centre Pompidou is open 12 noon to 10 pm every day except Tuesdays.
Saturday, Sunday, and holidays, 10 am to 10 pm.
Parking: entry from Rue des Halles, Rue Rambuteau, Rue de Turbigo
Metro stations: Rambuteau, Hôtel de Ville, Châtelet; RER Châtelet-les-Halles
Telephone: Information 277-1233; Programs 277-1112
Address: Centre national d'art et de Culture
         Georges Pompidou, 75191 Paris Cedex 04

C N A C is a bi-monthly magazine published by Centre Pompidou's Public Relations Department. It contains up to date detailed information on various programs and cultural events, with background information, interviews, and essays.

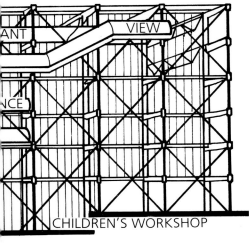

RESTAURANT

VIEW

ENTRANCE

CHILDREN'S WORKSHOP

Métro
Stations

Châtelet
Halles
Hôtel de Ville
Arts et Métiers
Rambuteau

Bus
Numbers
21, 29, 38, 47, 58,
67, 69, 70, 72, 74,
75, 76, 81, 85, 96

Centre
Pompidou

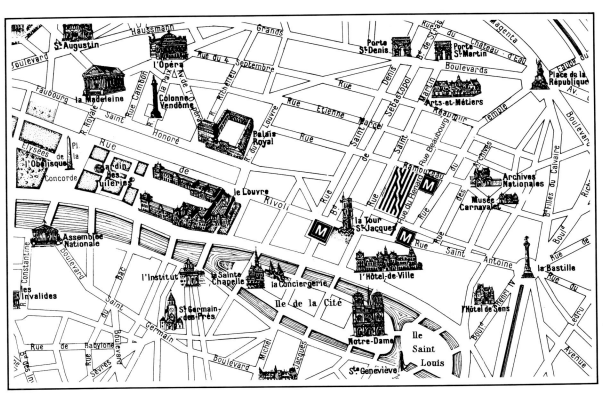

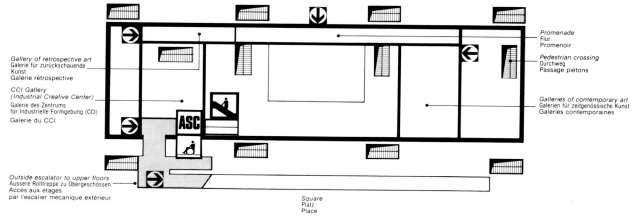

Gallery of retrospective art
Galerie für zurückschauende
Kunst
Galerie rétrospective

CCI Gallery
(Industrial Creative Center)
Galerie des Zentrums
für Industrielle Formgebung (CCI)
Galerie du CCI

Outside escalator to upper floors
Aussere Rolltreppe zu Obergeschössen
Accès aux étages
par l'escalier mécanique extérieur

Promenade
Flur
Promenoir

Pedestrian crossing
Durchweg
Passage piétons

Galleries of contemporary art
Galerien für zeitgenössische Kunst
Galeries contemporaines

Square
Platz
Place

ASC

Mezzanine . Zwischengeschoss . Mezzanine

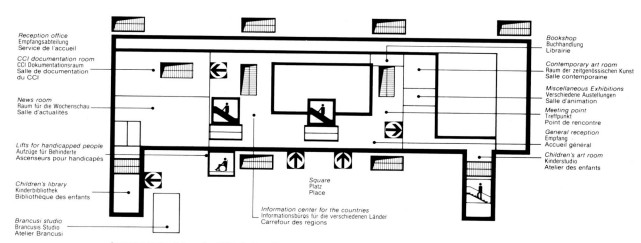

Reception office
Empfangsabteilung
Service de l'accueil

CCI documentation room
CCI Dokumentationsraum
Salle de documentation
du CCI

News room
Raum für die Wochenschau
Salle d'actualités

Lifts for handicapped people
Aufzüge für Behinderte
Ascenseurs pour handicapés

Children's library
Kinderbibliothek
Bibliothèque des enfants

Brancusi studio
Brancusis Studio
Atelier Brancusi

Bookshop
Buchhandlung
Librairie

Contemporary art room
Raum der zeitgenössischen Kunst
Salle contemporaine

Miscellaneous Exhibitions
Verschiedene Austellungen
Salle d'animation

Meeting point
Treffpunkt
Point de rencontre

General reception
Empfang
Accueil général

Children's art room
Kinderstudio
Atelier des enfants

Square
Platz
Place

Information center for the countries
Informationsbüros für die verschiedenen Länder
Carrefour des regions

General reception/Information/CCI . Empfang/CCI Informationshalle . Accueil général/Information/CCI

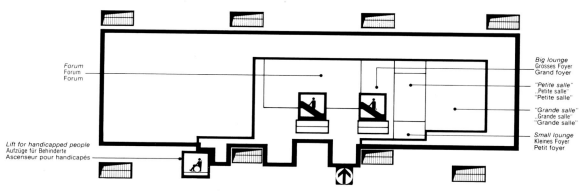

Forum
Forum
Forum

Lift for handicapped people
Aufzüge für Behinderte
Ascenseur pour handicapés

Big lounge
Grosses Foyer
Grand foyer

"Petite salle"
„Petite salle"
"Petite salle"

"Grande salle"
„Grande salle"
"Grande salle"

Small lounge
Kleines Foyer
Petit foyer

Forum/"Grande salle"/"Petite salle" . Forum/„Grande salle"/„Petite salle" . Forum/"Grande salle"/"Petite salle"

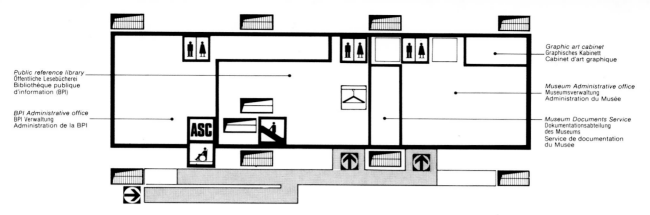

Public reference library
Öffentliche Lesebücherei
Bibliothèque publique
d'information (BPI)

BPI Administrative office
BPI Verwaltung
Administration de la BPI

Graphic art cabinet
Graphisches Kabinett
Cabinet d'art graphique

Museum Administrative office
Museumsverwaltung
Administration du Musée

Museum Documents Service
Dokumentationsabteilung
des Museums
Service de documentation
du Musée

ASC

2nd floor - Library entrance . Zweiter Stock - Bibliothekeingang . 2e étage - Entrée bibliothèque

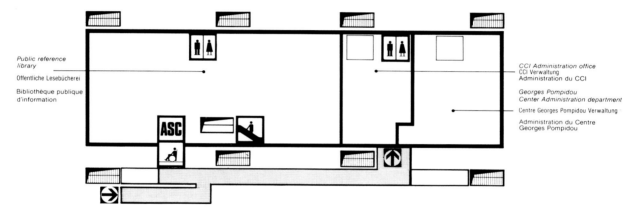

Public reference
library

Öffentliche Lesebücherei

Bibliothèque publique
d'information

CCI Administration office
CCI Verwaltung
Administration du CCI

Georges Pompidou
Center Administration department

Centre Georges Pompidou Verwaltung

Administration du Centre
Georges Pompidou

ASC

1st floor - Library . Erster Stock - Bibliothek . 1er étage - Bibliothèque

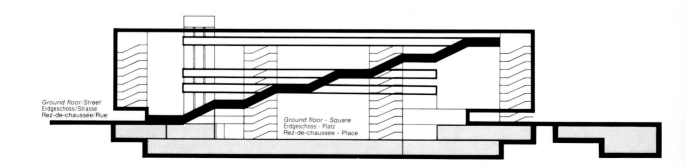

Ground floor/Street
Erdgeschoss/Strasse
Rez-de-chaussée/Rue

Ground floor - Square
Erdgeschoss - Platz
Rez-de-chaussée - Place

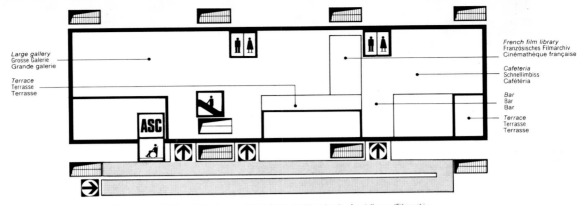

Large gallery
Grosse Galerie
Grande galerie

Terrace
Terrasse
Terrasse

French film library
Französisches Filmarchiv
Cinémathèque française

Cafeteria
Schnellimbiss
Cafétéria

Bar
Bar
Bar

Terrace
Terrasse
Terrasse

Fifth floor - Temporary exhibitions/Film library • Fünfter Stock - Vorübergehende Ausstellungen/Filmarchiv •
5e étage - Expositions temporaires/Cinémathèque

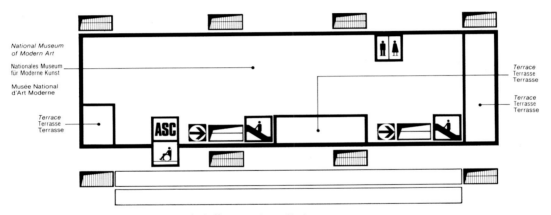

*National Museum
of Modern Art*

Nationales Museum
für Moderne Kunst

Musée National
d'Art Moderne

Terrace
Terrasse
Terrasse

Terrace
Terrasse
Terrasse

Terrace
Terrasse
Terrasse

Fourth floor - Museum • Vierter Stock - Museum • 4e étage - Musée

Permanent exhibition of the National Museum of Modern Art
Dauersammlungen des Nationalen Museums für Moderne Kunst
Collections permanentes du Musée National d'Art Moderne

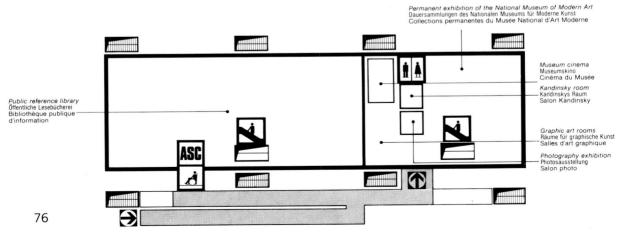

Museum cinema
Museumskino
Cinéma du Musée

Kandinsky room
Kandinskys Raum
Salon Kandinsky

Public reference library
Öffentliche Lesebücherei
Bibliothèque publique
d'information

Graphic art rooms
Räume für graphische Kunst
Salles d'art graphique

Photography exhibition
Photosausstellung
Salon photo

76

Third floor - Museum and library entrance • Dritter Stock - Eingang zu Museum und Bibliothek
3e étage - Entrée Musée/Bibliothèque

STATISTICS

Visitors

Total: 8,064,308 (for 1981); 7,775,890 (for 1980)
Average per day: 25,847 (for 1981); 24,923 (for 1980)
First time visitors: 25%; once a week: 29%; once a year: 20%; more than once a year:27%
Parisians: 44%; Paris region: 19%
Younger than 35 years of age: 81.3%; younger than 25: 54.5%; over 46: 10%
Students: 42.6%; Middle class: 35%
Male: 63.1%; Female: 36.8%
Length of average visit: one-and-a-half hours.
Busiest time: 2 - 6 p.m.

Cost

993 million French francs (approx. $200 million).
Annual operating cost: 217.5 million French francs (for 1981) and 210.1 million francs (for 1980).

National Museum of Modern Art (M.N.A.M.)

Collection contains 15,000 works of art (paintings, sculptures, prints and photographs).
Collection occupies 17,325m²
In 1981 it loaned 1,121 works (775 in France and 346 to foreign countries), organized 41 events (27 of them travelling exhibits), and held 21 meetings, 8 roundtable discussions and 22 lectures.
Its archives grow annually by thousands of slides, photographs, books, catalogues, magazines, and hundreds of newly-acquired works of art.

Public Information Library (B.P.I.)

Main library sits 1,300 visitors and the News Room sits 150.
Number of visitors in 1981: 4,422,062 to all its facilities (14,393 per day) and 3,271,121 to the library alone.
Length of average visit: 3 hours.
75% of visitors are young and unmarried, residents of Paris and its region; 50% are students.
58% come with a specific goal. The most popular subjects are Economy, Business Administration, Marketing and the Social Sciences.
65% of the books are in French, 18% in English, 5% in German, 4% in Spanish, and 1.6% in the Slavic languages.
12.5% of users consult the foreign languages collection.
Number of visitors to the Children's Library: 109,062 (for 1981), an average of 400 per day.

Industrial Age Design Center (C.C.I.)

Visitors number from 700 to 1,000 daily
Its library contains about 10,000 books, and receives regularly more than 500 magazines and journals in both French and foreign languages.
It has a collection of over 36,000 slides, 20,000 black & white photographs, and an annual growth of 10,000 additional references.

The Music Research Center (I.R.C.A.M.)

Contains: 7 studios, 1 anechoic chamber, 1 computer room, 6 laboratories, 1 conference room, 1 library, 32 offices, 1 mechanical workshop, 1 experimental performance hall (seating 400)

POMPIDOU CENTER
Photography by Jeremiah Bragstad
Text by Ivan Žaknić

Additional photography by
LAURENT ROUSSEAU
and others mentioned herein.

The map on page 73
is the courtesy of:
Librairie Arthaud.
The plans on pages 74, 75 & 76
are the courtesy of:
Document OTUA, Paris and
Dessins Studio Jean-Pierre Thérond.

Edited and produced by
Richard Schuettge
458 Gravatt
Berkeley, California 94705

Typography by Jennifer Tayloe
Design by Wendy Calmenson
Printing by the Dai Nippon Printing Company

Printed in Japan

FLAMMARION DISTRIBUTORS
ISBN 2.08.012007.7